W9-BUA-477

EASY SIMULATIONS
CIVIL WAR

by Tim Bailey

New York • Toronto • London • Auckland • Sydney
Mexico City • New Delhi • Hong Kong • Buenos Aires

Teaching
Resources

DEDICATION

To my friends, colleagues, and family, thanks!

ACKNOWLEDGMENTS

To Maria L. Chang and the rest of the talented and dedicated staff from
Scholastic Teaching Resources, thanks!

Editor: Maria L. Chang
Cover design by Jason Robinson
Cover illustration by Doug Knutson
Interior design by Holly Grundon
Interior illustrations by Mona Mark
Map by Jim McMahon

ISBN-13: 978-0-439-52219-9
ISBN-10: 0-439-52219-6
Copyright © 2008 by Tim Bailey

CONTENTS

Introduction

August 24, 1862

Dear Ayleah, my sister,

Today, right at dawn, the cannons started pouring on us. I have missed you. This

war has been long and hard. I want you to tell the family that I am now too injured

to fight and I may be blind . . .

This quote is taken from a letter, not by a real soldier fighting in the Civil War, but by Adriana, a fifth-grade student in my class who was role-playing a 1st private in the Confederate army, wounded at a reenactment of a battle during our weeklong simulation. Using simulations in the classroom is one of the most powerful teaching methods you can choose. Students learn most when they see a purpose to an activity, are engaged in the learning process, and are having fun. Children love to role-play, and they do it naturally. How often have you overheard them say something like, "Okay, you be the bad guy, and I'll be the good guy"? Why not tap into students' imaginations and creativity and teach them by engaging them in a simulation?

What Is a Simulation?

A simulation is a teacher-directed, student-driven activity that provides lifelike problem-solving experiences through role-playing or reenacting. Simulations use an incredible range of effective teaching strategies. Students will acquire a rich and deep understanding of history that is impossible to gain through the use of any textbook. They will take responsibility for their own learning, discover that they must work cooperatively with their team in order to succeed, and learn that they must apply skills in logic to solve the problems they encounter. You will find that this simulation addresses a variety of academic content areas and fully integrates them into this social studies activity. In addition, simulations motivate *all* of your students to participate because what they're required to do will be fully supported by their teammates and you.

History Comes Alive

Easy Simulations: Civil War is designed to teach students about this critical period in American history by inviting them to relive some of the events of this period. Over the course of five days, they will re-create some of the experiences of the people who were living in a nation at war with itself. By taking the perspective of a historical character living through the war, students will see that history is so much more than just names, dates, and places, but rather the real experiences of people like themselves.

Students must work together in groups and use their problem-solving skills to deal with challenges they face as soldiers fighting in the Civil War. Throughout the simulation, students will keep a journal of their experiences. At the end of the simulation, they will write a final journal entry describing what they have experienced and learned from the activity. You can use this journal as an assessment tool to determine how much students have learned.

Everything You Need

This book provides an easy-to-use guide for running this five-day simulation—everything you need to create an educational experience that your students will talk about for a very long time. You will find background information for both yourself and your students, describing the history and significance of the Civil War. You'll also find authentic accounts—letters and journals— written by people who experienced the same trials that your students will be enduring, as well as a map, tables, illustrations, and reproducible student journal pages.

> **B**efore you begin the simulation, be certain to read through the entire book so you can familiarize yourself with how a simulation works and prepare any materials that you may need. Feel free to supplement with photos, illustrations, diaries, videos, music, and any other details that will enhance the experience for you and your students. Enjoy!

SETTING THE SCENE:
THE AMERICAN CIVIL WAR

From April 1861 until April 1865, the United States of America was engaged in the deadliest war it has ever fought—with itself. The War Between the States claimed the lives of some 620,000 men; nearly as many soldiers as have died in all of America's other wars combined, from the American Revolution through the war in Iraq. Two percent of America's population perished in those four years of war.

The history of the Civil War goes back much further than 1861. Thomas Jefferson, when forced to delete antislavery language from the Declaration of Independence in 1776, predicted that a civil war would be fought in America over the issue. In 1777, under the Articles of Confederation, the United States's first national government failed because of the issue of states' rights versus federal power. Many northern states favored a strong, central federal government, while the majority of southern states wanted more power left to the states' control.

The divisions between the North and South went deep. The South saw the North as industrial and overbearing, unable to understand the agricultural South. The North regarded the South as backward slavers, stuck in the ways of the past. Although Congress tried to reach compromises on the issues of states' rights and slavery, the tension continued to build.

The animosity of the southern states toward their northern neighbors finally boiled over with the election of Abraham Lincoln on November 6, 1860. The South viewed Lincoln as antislavery and pro–federal government. His election prompted South Carolina to secede from the United States on December 20 of that same year, declaring: "*We, the people of the state of South Carolina, in Convention assembled, do declare and ordain . . . that the union now subsisting between South Carolina and the other States under the United States of America is hereby dissolved.*" By February 1861, six more southern states had joined South Carolina to form their own country called the Confederate States of America and had elected Jefferson Davis as its first president. By the end of the Civil War, a total of eleven states would become a part of the Confederate States of America.

President Abraham Lincoln and the United States government did not recognize the Confederate States of America as a legitimate new country. In his inaugural address in January 1861, Lincoln proclaimed that "*no state, upon its own mere motion, can lawfully get out of the Union. . . . They can only do so against the law, and by revolution.*" Lincoln knew that the United States of America could not survive the

Easy Simulations: Civil War © 2008 by Tim Bailey, Scholastic Teaching Resources

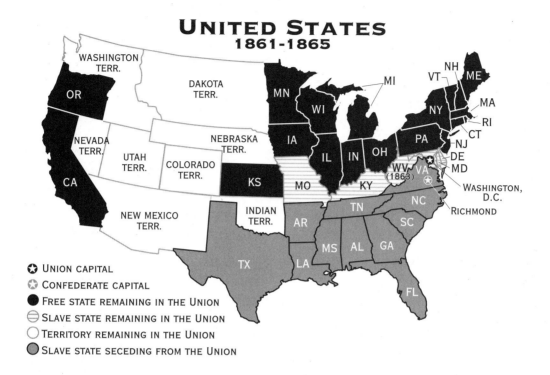

division that was taking place between the states, and he expressed that belief when he said, "*A house divided against itself cannot stand.*" He was prepared to fight in order to preserve the Union. The South was ready to fight to preserve their way of life. That fight began on April 12, 1861, at Fort Sumter in Charleston Harbor, South Carolina.

The first battle of the Civil War did not claim any lives, but it did incite men on both sides to volunteer to fight in the war. War fever gripped both the North and the South. Men joined the army for the glory and adventure they thought the war would bring. John W. Stevens, a confederate recruit from Texas wrote: "*Our patriotism was just bubbling up and boiling over and frying and fizzling.*" Both sides anticipated a very short war with victory for their side.

The grand and glorious illusions of war died in the summer of 1861 at the first real battle of the Civil War. That battle is known by two names: 1st Battle of Manassas and 1st Battle of Bull Run. (The Union Army named battles for the nearest body of water—in this case, a small river called Bull Run. The Confederacy named battles after the nearest town, such as Manassas.) The battle took place just outside of Washington, D.C. The South felt confident that it could capture the nation's capital and force the Union to concede, while the North was convinced that its army would put the rebels in their place, forcing a quick surrender by the South. So confident were the Northerners that a number of civilians and reporters from the capital city went out with picnic baskets in their carriages to watch the battle. However, when the South soundly defeated the raw Northern recruits, these sightseers speedily scrambled back to Washington, D.C., and their illusions of a swift victory lay on the battlefield along with more than 5,000 casualties from both sides. Although the South had won the first battle of the war, they had neither the manpower nor resources to press their advantage, and the Civil War ground on for years. Thousands of men died in battle after battle. The Battle of Gettysburg alone produced more than 50,000 casualties after only three days of fighting.

The Confederacy, under the brilliant military leadership of General Robert E. Lee and his capable commanders, won the majority of battles as the North struggled to find sound military leadership. Although the South was victorious in the field, they could not win the economic war against the industrial North. At the beginning of the war the South had no industrial base or major railroads and, of the 9 million people living in the Confederacy, 3.5 million were slaves. On the other hand, the North had nearly 22 million citizens and was heavily industrialized with a solid economy. For every two soldiers that the Confederacy could field, the Union could field five. And the factories of the North could turn out war supplies faster than the South could destroy them.

As the war dragged on, the North relied on Lincoln's "Anaconda Plan," strangling the South economically with blockades and controlling trade on the Mississippi River. This strategy took a huge toll on the South, and the rebels literally ran out of the supplies necessary to fight a war as well as the basic necessities for its citizens.

The war did not end abruptly; it ground to a halt as the South ran out of men, food, and war supplies. On April 9, 1865, General Ulysses S. Grant accepted General Lee's surrender at Appomattox Station, Virginia. General Grant would later write: *My own feelings . . . were sad and depressed. I felt like anything rather than rejoicing at the downfall of a foe who had fought so long and so valiantly, and had suffered so much.*

Abraham Lincoln had a vision for rebuilding the South and welcoming these states back into the Union. He voiced his opinion in his second inaugural speech: *"With malice for none; with charity for all . . ."* But Lincoln would not witness the reconstruction of the South. John Wilkes Booth assassinated the president only five days after Lee's surrender in Virginia.

The American Civil War introduced many changes in how wars were fought. New technologies such as submarines, land mines, trench warfare, iron-clad warships, aerial reconnaissance, and many other innovations came about because of the war.

Most significantly, as a result of the war, black slaves in the South had been freed, even though they continued to suffer decades of injustice. The Civil War pitted brother against brother, literally and figuratively. But it is in the words of Lincoln in the Gettysburg Address where we find a reason for the bloodshed: "*. . . we here highly resolve that these dead shall not have died in vain; that this nation, under God, shall have a new birth of freedom; and that government of the people, by the people, for the people, shall not perish from the earth.*"

Easy Simulations: Civil War © 2008 by Tim Bailey, Scholastic Teaching Resources

Before You Start

Organizing and Managing the Simulation

Before students embark on their five-day adventure, you will need to set the stage for the simulation. First, make photocopies of the reproducible pages at the end of this section:

- Being a Soldier in the Civil War (pages 17–19)

- Choose a Role: The North (page 20)

- Choose a Role: The South (page 21)

- A Soldier's Journal (pages 22–24)

- Equipment and Supplies for the Union Army (page 25)

- Equipment and Supplies for the Confederate Army (page 26)

- Minor Injury Table (page 27)

- Major Injury Table (page 28)

- Infection Table (page 29)

- Disease Table (page 30)

- Morale Table (page 31)

- Rubrics (page 32)

- Simulation spinner (page 33)

Explain to students that they will be re-creating history, using the simulation and their imaginations to experience what it was like to be a soldier during the Civil War. They will be taking on the roles of various citizens in that period and facing the same decisions that those people faced. Emphasize that the decisions they make will determine whether they survive the bloodiest conflict in American history or end up in a shallow grave on a war-torn battlefield.

Distribute copies of "Being a Soldier in the Civil War" to students. You might also want to reproduce the pages on transparencies to display on an overhead projector. As a class, read the selection to build students' background knowledge about the period they're about to live through. Then divide the class into groups of four or five students. These student groups will be working together throughout the simulation, so members will need to be seated together during the activity. Assign half of the groups to be units of Union soldiers, and the other half to be units of Confederate soldiers.

Choosing a Role

After you have divided the class into small groups, distribute the "Choose a Role" handouts (for North and South), which describe the various roles students can play during the simulation. Invite students to select a role from the handout, explaining the differences in background between the Northern and the Southern soldiers. Each role comes with its own set of special skills and with strengths and weaknesses indicated by a number ranging from 1 to 5. These numbers are called "attributes." The higher the attribute number, the more able the character (see Attributes, below).

Students should pay special attention to the Morale and Health attributes. The Morale number indicates how confident and spirited a soldier is, while the Health number shows how healthy a person is—5 is perfect health, and 0 is dead. These numbers can change throughout the simulation.

Encourage students within each group to choose a variety of roles to make the simulation more interesting. While any combination of roles is possible within each group, it may not be wise to have a group of, say, five farmers in a military unit. After students have chosen a role to play in the simulation, they will outfit their characters and go through basic training to become soldiers in Episode 1.

Attributes

Attributes are the numbers that make each soldier role unique. The attributes are Strength, Common Sense, Stamina, Marksmanship, Agility, Medical Expertise, Morale, and Health. Throughout the simulation, attribute numbers will be used during "skill spins" to resolve various situations that the soldiers encounter. Students will spin the spinner (or roll a number cube) and compare the number they've spun to their attribute number to determine whether their attempt at solving a problem is successful or not. For example, say a unit is trying to dig in for cover during a battle in the simulation. In order to dig in successfully, a unit soldier (a student) must make a spin and compare that number to his Strength attribute. If the number he spins is equal to or lower than his Strength attribute, then he has enough Strength to successfully dig in for cover. If the number spun is higher than the Strength attribute, then his Strength was insufficient and he has failed. Each unit member is allowed only one skill spin per situation. In other words, if a student fails in his Strength spin, he cannot attempt to dig in again. Someone else in the unit would have to try her luck by making another Strength spin.

Below is a description of the various attributes:

Strength: The physical strength of a person. This determines how much a soldier can carry without becoming fatigued and how easily he or she performs tasks that require physical power.

Common Sense: A person's wisdom and ability to understand and reason. This can be very important in figuring out how to react to different situations and foreseeing problems.

Stamina: How much physical and mental endurance a person has—for instance, how long someone can march or move without sleep.

Marksmanship: How skilled a person is at shooting. A low number indicates a very poor shot, while a high number signifies a sharpshooter.

Agility: A person's dexterity and speed. Successfully running for cover or hiding in the woods may depend on this number.

Medical Expertise: How skilled a person is at caring for the sick and injured. A high number in this attribute may save the life of another soldier in the unit.

Morale: This number represents the emotional state of a soldier. A high number indicates a soldier in good spirits, ready to charge into battle and defeat the enemy. A low number signifies a soldier who just wants to go home and is likely to break and run when the fighting starts. All soldiers start with a Morale of 5.

Health: A person's current health. All soldiers start with a Health of 5, which indicates perfect health. If the number slides to 0, the soldier has died. Health can go down either from being wounded or from disease. The only way to regain lost Health points is to have someone in the soldier's unit make a successful Medical Expertise spin. The Health number, however, can never go above 5. Each scenario describes when a Medical Expertise spin may be made. If a soldier dies at some point during the simulation, that student should still participate in group decisions and discussions as the "unseen conscious" of the unit. That student should still be expected to keep up his or her soldier journal.

Keeping a Journal

After students have chosen their roles, distribute copies of "A Soldier's Journal" —one copy of the cover page and "Equipment and Supplies" page and six copies of the blank Dear Diary page. Explain to students that they will be recording their experiences during the simulation in their journals on a daily basis. To give the journals a more realistic look, have students make a cover, using a sheet of 12-by-18-inch brown construction paper or a large brown paper grocery bag. Demonstrate how to "sew" the journal pages inside the cover page using a hole punch and yarn, as shown.

Name: _____ Date: _____

Student Page

A SOLDIER'S JOURNAL

Soldier's Name: ___Robert Jones___

Soldier's Role and Rank: ___Farmer / Sergeant___

Serving in the Army of the (circle one): (Union)   Confederacy

Assigned Unit: ___10th Ohio Infantry___

Soldier's Attributes:

Strength: ___4___

Common Sense: ___3___

Stamina: ___4___

Marksmanship: ___4___

Agility: ___3___

Medical Expertise: ___2___

Health*: ___5___

Morale*: ___5___

*These numbers may be adjusted throughout the simulation.

22   *Easy Simulations: Civil War*

On the cover page, have students fill in the information about the character they've chosen—their name, role and rank, allegiance (Union or Confederacy), unit name, and attribute numbers. When students fill in their journal pages, have them record the date of the simulation, not the actual date. For example, use June 9, 1862, rather than May 11, 2008. Students should record the events that took place in that day's episode. Encourage them to write their journal entry "in character," as if the events had really happened to them. This activity gives students the opportunity to take on another person's perspective and experience history "firsthand."

A student's journal often yields rich insights into the student's understanding of historical events and how they affected ordinary citizens' lives. Use these journals as your primary tool for assessing students' participation and evaluating how well they understand the simulation's content. (See Assessing and Evaluating, page 15.)

Equipment and Supplies

Hand out copies of the "Equipment and Supplies" lists to students. Note that there are two lists—one for Union soldiers and another for Confederates. Each list contains items that soldiers may choose to carry with them. Some of the items are valuable, and some will turn out to be useless, as the real soldiers discovered in the war. Students may select as much or as little as they wish; however, they *must* take a uniform, a weapon, provisions, and ammunition. The kind of weapon a soldier gets and the quality of food a unit receives are determined during the first episode.

After choosing their equipment and supplies, have students record them on the "Equipment and Supplies" page of their journal. Next, students will need to total the weight of what they are carrying. A person can comfortably carry 10 pounds for every Strength point. For instance, a Farmer has a Strength of 4 so he can carry up to 40 pounds without a problem. However, if the weight carried exceeds the Strength limit of a soldier, up to a maximum of 10 extra pounds, he must make Stamina checks during the simulation at a −1 modifier. For example, the simulation calls for soldiers to make a 30-mile march. During the march they must make a skill spin on their Stamina number. Normally, a Farmer has a Stamina of 4 and so a spin of 4 or less would be successful. But if the Farmer is carrying extra weight, he must subtract 1 from his Stamina number before making the spin. Now he must spin a 3 or less to be successful. If the spin fails, he loses one Morale point.

Name: _____ Date: _____

Student Page

EQUIPMENT AND SUPPLIES

Soldier's Name and Rank: Sergeant Robert Jones

Weapon (circle one): Terrible   Poor   (Good)   Excellent

Provisions (circle one): Terrible   Poor   (Good)   Excellent

Equipment (Add the weight carried): _____
Weapon (10 lbs),
wool uniform (7 lbs),
ammunition (3 lbs),
provisions (10 lbs)
shelter tent (8 lbs),
haversack (2 lbs)

Strength: 4   x 10 = 40   Total Weight: 40

*If the Total Weight is greater than the Strength x 10 number, there is a −1 Stamina penalty.

Conducting the Simulation

This simulation is divided into five episodes—one for each day of the school week—each re-creating the challenges and experiences of being a soldier during the War Between the States. An episode should take about 45–60 minutes, depending on your class size. Consider starting the actual simulation on a Monday so that it will run its course by Friday. Complete all preparatory work (e.g., building background knowledge, choosing a character, etc.) during the previous week.

Each episode consists of two scenarios, which feature problem-solving activities that simulate some of the difficulties and experiences that soldiers of the Union and Confederacy faced. How well students negotiate these challenges, and, as in any war, how lucky they are, will determine whether they survive the experience. At the end of the simulation, students will engage in a discussion and debriefing of the simulation experience.

A Sample Scenario

The scenario presented in each episode is where students actually get to participate in a historical event. Below is an abbreviated version of a scenario in Episode 3 that demonstrates how a simulation is typically run.

Have each unit stand in separate areas of the classroom. Describe the scene in which the soldiers are walking down a quiet tree-lined country road in rural Virginia in late June of 1862. Suddenly they hear someone coming toward them from around a bend in the road. They know that the enemy lines lie in that direction, but they cannot see who is coming due to the trees and underbrush. Read the three options available to the soldiers:

1. Load your weapons and fire at the approaching sound.

2. Hide off to the side of the road and wait to see who it is.

3. Send one of your soldiers up ahead to try and find out who is coming.

Allow students within each unit to discuss their next step, then invite a spokesperson to present the group's decision. (Choose a different spokesperson from each unit every day.)

Teacher: Okay, has everyone had enough time to decide what they want to do? Great, 53rd Alabama Infantry, what did you decide?

53rd Alabama Spokesperson: We decided to send someone to see who is coming.

Teacher: All right, who are you sending?

53rd Alabama Spokesperson: Sam. He wants to go find out what it is.

Teacher: Okay. *(Notes on a piece of paper that the 53rd sends Sam to scout)* 35th Virginia?

35th Virginia Spokesperson: Yeah, we'll do that, too. We are sending Alicia.

Teacher: You're sending Alicia to scout? Okay. *(Makes a note of that)* 10th Ohio?

10th Ohio Spokesperson: We are going to hide in the bushes and see who is coming.

51st New York Spokesperson: We want to do that, too.

Teacher: All right, both the 10th Ohio and the 51st New York want to hide and see what is coming down the road. *(Makes note of these decisions)* 15th Maine, you are last. What did you decide to do?

15th Maine Spokesperson: We aren't going to take any chances. We are going to blast whatever is coming around the bend.

Teacher: Okay. Erase one round of ammunition from the cartridges on your supply sheet. *(The students adjust the amount of ammunition that they are carrying, and the teacher notes the group's decision to fire at the noise.)* Now let's see what happened because of your decisions. Let's start with the 53rd Alabama. Sam, you need to spin your Agility number or lower in order to sneak up on whatever is coming down the road and not be seen.

Sam: I should have let Kyle scout up ahead. He has a higher Agility number.

Teacher: Too late now. Go ahead and spin. *(Sam spins a 5, which is higher than his Agility number of 3. Sam and his group groan.)* As you try and sneak through the woods you trip over a tree branch and fall crashing to the ground. *(The teacher now role-plays an old farmer who is heading down the road with his cow.)* "Eh, what was that? Who is in those woods? Come on out or I'll take my stick to you!" He is waving a walking stick in the direction of the woods.

Sam: I'm going to go back and tell the rest of the regiment that it is just an old man and a cow.

15th Maine Spokesperson: Oh no! I hope we didn't shoot the old man and his cow!

Teacher: Well, I guess we will find that out when we get to your turn. Now, 35th Virginia, it's your turn. Alicia, make an Agility spin . . .

This is how the scenarios will typically run, with role-playing students dealing with the situations that confront them, and you, the teacher, acting out all the other parts while coordinating the simulation. Present the situation in the scenario to students and then give them time to make their decisions. You have to stay on your toes because students may come up with a solution different from those offered in the simulation. In such cases, you can either wing it and accommodate them or tell them that they must stick to the options offered in the simulation. Do not reveal the outcome of each student's or group's decision until everyone has responded; only then do you respond to each person or group as the rest of the class observes the outcome of the choices as scripted in the scenario.

Injury, Disease, and Infection Tables

Needless to say, war is a dangerous business. The two key factors that will determine the success or failure of a unit are the Morale and Health of the soldiers in that regiment. Many factors during the simulation can raise or lower these two important numbers. During the course of the simulation, students will be asked to make a variety of skill spins to determine the consequences of their choices. If the skill spin fails (a number higher than the skill number is spun), then you will have to consult one of the following tables and soldiers will have to make another spin to determine the outcome of the first failed spin.

- Minor Injury Table (page 27)
- Major Injury Table (page 28)
- Infection Table (page 29)
- Disease Table (page 30)
- Morale Table (page 31)

For example, during a battle soldiers may be directed to make an Agility spin in order to run for cover without getting shot. Say a soldier spins a number higher than her Agility number and is hit by enemy fire. Now she must spin again to see if the wound is minor or major.

- If she spins any number from 1 to 4, the wound is minor.
- A spin of 5 or 6 means the wound is major.

Any consequence of spinning on these tables is applied to the soldier immediately. The use of these tables is dictated by what is happening in a scenario. You will be directed when to consult the different tables.

Assessing and Evaluating

Throughout the simulation students should be evaluated on their historical understanding. You can do this by assessing the authenticity and historical accuracy of the way they play their character and the journal entries they've written throughout this simulation.

Use the rubrics on page 32 to give each student a daily score, based on the student's journal entries and your observations. Each rubric is scored on a scale of 1 to 5, with 1 being the lowest possible score and 5 the highest. Add the two scores to generate a number from 2 to 10. To convert this total score to a percentage score, multiply the total score by 10. You can award scores such as 4.5 if you feel a student was at least a 4 but not quite a 5. This daily percentage score can then be averaged over the week to generate an individual score for each student.

	Student Journal		Teacher Observations		Score Percentage
Monday	3	+	4	x 10	70%
Tuesday	4	+	4	x 10	80%
Wednesday	3.5	+	5	x 10	85%
Thursday	2.5	+	4	x 10	65%
Friday	4	+	5	x 10	90%
Average for the week					78%

Another piece of the assessment puzzle is the group dynamic. This simulation is the perfect setting for teaching students the value of teamwork and collaboration. At the end of each day's simulation, as students are recording in their journals, debrief quickly with each group to discuss how they had worked together as a group. Were they patient with each other? Were they respectful of each other's opinions? Did the group dynamic feel supportive or combative? Based on this discussion, use Rubric #3 to record a group score for that day.

At the end of the week, total the group score and then multiply by 4 in order to give the group a percentile score. After the simulation is finished, combine the group's scores with each member's daily scores to give each student a final grade for the simulation. For example, one group's scores might be as follows:

	Group's Daily Score
Monday	4
Tuesday	4
Wednesday	5
Thursday	3
Friday	5
Total	21 x 4 = 84%

A student with an individual score of 78% combined with his group score of 84% will get a final average score for the simulation of 81%, or a B.

BEING A SOLDIER IN THE CIVIL WAR

At the commencement of the war there was in vogue an order from the War Department prohibiting the enlistment of any into the army who was not in stature at least Five feet and Six inches in height. I was short by just One Half Inch . . . and the fact caused me many anxious hours. [But when my company was mustered in], with a brick in my hand I fell into the rear rank, not at the end but near it [with] a man on my right and another on my left. The brick was under my heels but buried in the straw out of sight. This made me two inches higher when standing on my tiptoes: made me up to the required standard.

—W. H. H. Barker, volunteer from Iowa

At the beginning of the Civil War, men from both sides were eager to enlist in the military. They believed that the war would be short. This was a chance for glory and adventure, and if they didn't volunteer, they would miss out on the opportunity of a lifetime. Families encouraged their young men to volunteer for the army, and young women like Virginian Fannie Beers felt that "*the Confederate gray [uniform] was a thing of beauty, the outer garb of true and noble souls. Every man who wore it became ennobled in the eyes of every woman.*" In the North it was the same story. "*All of the girls came up to see us sworn in. We had fine times that day,*" wrote Jason L. Ellis, a volunteer with the 18th Iowa Infantry.

The men from both North and South who volunteered to join the army were not professional soldiers. They were farmers, lawyers, and shopkeepers. The Union volunteers were nicknamed Billy Yank by the Southerners, and the Confederate soldiers were called Johnny Reb by the Northerners. By the end of the war, soldiers serving in the armies of the North and South ranged in age from 10 to 73 years. They were all Americans willing to die for their country.

The soldiers of the South had some advantages over their Northern counterparts. Most of the soldiers from the South lived in the country and knew how to shoot, ride a horse, and live in the wild.

Easy Simulations: Civil War © 2008 by Tim Bailey, Scholastic Teaching Resources

(continued)

Being a Soldier in the Civil War *(continued)*

Many of the Northern soldiers lived in the cities and worked in factories. They didn't know how to shoot a gun. However, the Union soldiers were much better supplied than the Confederate soldiers. Many Southern soldiers fought without shoes or boots, even in winter! The factories of the North could furnish more provisions and make better weapons. Most important, the North could recruit more men into the army than could the Confederacy.

Once a man joined the army, he quickly learned that a soldier's life is not one of grand adventure, but of hard work, followed by periods of mind-numbing boredom and interrupted by moments of sheer terror. A Union volunteer, Warren Lee Goss, wrote, *"It takes a raw recruit some time to learn that he is not to think or suggest, but obey. I acquired it at last, in humility and mud, but it was tough."* The Civil War soldier marched into battle elbow-to-elbow with his fellow soldiers and, as the soldiers around him fell from enemy fire, he would step into their place and keep marching toward the enemy. This kind of discipline under fire was an essential part of a soldier's basic training, which included learning to shoot, maneuver on a battlefield, dig trenches, care for each others' injuries, and many other soldiering skills. Pennsylvania volunteer Oliver Wilcox Norton describes how all of these skills were learned by new soldiers: *"The first thing in the morning is drill, then drill, then drill again. Then drill, drill, a little more drill. Then drill, and lastly drill. Between drills, we drill, and sometimes stop to eat a little and have roll call."*

After the soldiers were trained, things became much worse as they went off "to see the elephant," a popular phrase at the time that meant "to be in a real battle." The fresh food that they enjoyed at basic training was replaced by *salt horse*—a slang term for beef so heavily salted it was said to last for two years without rotting—and *desiccated vegetables*—slabs of heavily peppered dried vegetables, which were broken into chunks and tossed into boiling water to make a kind of soup. The most infamous of all the provisions that a Civil War soldier endured was *hard tack*—a simple flour-and-water biscuit baked to the consistency of concrete.

Of course, a soldier's purpose is to fight and defeat the enemy. The average Civil War soldier, if he lived long enough, saw a great deal of fighting. A private in the 20th Maine gave a vivid account of the sounds of battle: *"The air was filled with a medley of sounds, shouts, cheers, commands, oaths, the sharp report of rifles, the hissing shot, groans and prayers."* It wasn't until someone was trying to kill you that you knew how you would react under fire. Private Oliver Norton of the 83rd Pennsylvania watched his friends dying around him in battle and wrote, *"I snatched up a gun from the hands of a man who was shot through the head. Then I jumped over dead men with as little feeling as I would over a log. The feeling that was uppermost in my mind was a desire to kill as many rebels as I could. The loss of comrades maddened me."*

Whether or not one survived battle was as much a matter of luck as it was skill. If one was not killed outright on the battlefield, as were more than 200,000 soldiers, then he might very well be one of over 400,000 who died of either infections or disease.

Easy Simulations: Civil War © 2008 by Tim Bailey, Scholastic Teaching Resources

(continued)

Battlefield medicine was crude by today's standards. Thousands of maimed soldiers overwhelmed the few doctors who tried to care for the injured. Amputations were a very common way to deal with limbs that had been mangled by soft lead bullets and cannon balls. In addition, lack of proper hygiene—for example, doctors dropping surgical instruments and then wiping them off on their pants before continuing the operation—led to many instances of fatal infections.

Diseases were also a major killer of soldiers. As in any war, lack of clean water to drink and decent food to eat led to diseases like dysentery and typhoid fever. Infectious diseases, such as tuberculosis, measles, small pox, and others, killed thousands of soldiers. Entire regiments were unfit for battle because of diseases running rampant through their camps. Jason Ellis, one of the soldiers quoted earlier, survived two skirmishes and a major battle without a scratch only to die from a disease in 1863.

Soldiers who survived The War Between the States returned home and tried to rebuild their lives back in the "real world." Confederate General John C. Breckinridge remarked, "*I have asked myself more than once tonight: 'Are you the same man who stood gazing down on the faces of the dead on that awful battlefield; the soldiers lying there . . . with their eyes wide open? Is this the same world?'*"

Name: _____   Date: _____

CHOOSE A ROLE: THE NORTH

Directions: Select the role that you would like to play during the Civil War simulation. Record your choice and your attributes in your journal.

Roles	Strength	Common Sense	Stamina	Marksman-ship	Agility	Medical Expertise
Farmer	4	3	4	4	3	2
Tradesman	5	2	4	3	4	2
Former Slave	5	3	5	2	4	1
Factory Worker	3	3	3	3	4	4
Professional	2	4	2	4	3	5

Farmer – You grow a fairly small crop to feed your family and still have enough to sell for the rest of your family's needs. Like most Northern farmers, you are not well educated but know how to live off the land.

Tradesman – You are a skilled craftsman who specializes in working with metal or wood. (A tradesman could be a blacksmith or a carpenter.) Tradesmen are growing scarce as factories begin to replace the need for a tradesman's services.

Former Slave – You escaped slavery in the South using the Underground Railroad and have decided to fight for the freedom of the other slaves still in bondage.

Factory Worker – You live in the growing cities of the industrial northeastern United States. Industrial manufacturers employ thousands of workers, who create a great variety of goods.

Professional – Like the lawyers, doctors, teachers, and other well-educated people living throughout the North, you volunteered to fight for the principles that you believe in.

Easy Simulations: Civil War © 2008 by Tim Bailey, Scholastic Teaching Resources

CHOOSE A ROLE: THE SOUTH

Directions: Select the role that you would like to play during the Civil War simulation. Record your choice and your attributes in your journal.

Roles	Strength	Common Sense	Stamina	Marksman-ship	Agility	Medical Expertise
Farmer	4	3	4	4	3	2
Tradesman	5	2	4	4	3	2
Overseer	4	3	3	4	3	3
Dockworker	5	2	5	4	2	2
Aristocrat	2	3	3	5	3	4

Farmer – The vast majority of farmers in the South do not live on huge plantations and own hundreds of slaves. Like most Southern farmers, you grow enough to provide for your family, plus a little extra to sell at market.

Tradesman – As a carpenter or blacksmith, you are very important in the South. Because there's a lack of factories producing manufactured goods, the items you make from metal and wood are in high demand.

Overseer – Your job is to manage, or oversee, slaves. Plantation owners rely on overseers to keep the slaves under control and working hard.

Dockworker – You are a laborer at one of the many port cities of the South. You are strong and can work long hours without tiring.

Aristocrat – You are a wealthy member of the southern upper class. Well-educated, probably in Europe, you are one of the plantation growers and slave owners of the South.

Name: _____   Date: _____

A SOLDIER'S JOURNAL

Soldier's Name: _____

Soldier's Role and Rank: _____

Serving in the Army of the (circle one):   Union   Confederacy

Assigned Unit: _____

Soldier's Attributes:

Strength: _____

Common Sense: _____

Stamina: _____

Marksmanship: _____

Agility: _____

Medical Expertise: _____

Health*: _____

Morale*: _____

*These numbers may be adjusted throughout the simulation.

Easy Simulations: Civil War © 2008 by Tim Bailey, Scholastic Teaching Resources

Name: _____   Date: _____

EQUIPMENT AND SUPPLIES

Soldier's Name and Rank: _____

Weapon (circle one):	Terrible	Poor	Good	Excellent

Provisions (circle one):	Terrible	Poor	Good	Excellent

Equipment (Add the weight carried): _____

_____

_____

_____

_____

_____

_____

_____

Strength: _____ x 10 = _____   Total Weight: _____

*If the Total Weight is greater than the Strength x 10 number, there is a −1 Stamina penalty.

Name: _____ Date: _____

Date _____

Dear Diary,

_____

_____

_____

_____

_____

_____

_____

_____

_____

_____

_____

_____

_____

Easy Simulations: Civil War © 2008 by Tim Bailey, Scholastic Teaching Resources

EQUIPMENT AND SUPPLIES FOR THE UNION ARMY

*Weapons – 10 lbs
The weapon you get is determined during Episode 1.

> **Excellent:** Springfield Rifle
> Powerful, long-range rifle
>
> > (+1 to Marksmanship)
>
> **Good:** Enfield Rifle
> Well-made and reliable rifle
>
> > (+0 to Marksmanship)
>
> **Poor:** 1842 Smoothbore Musket
> 20-year-old musket
>
> > (–1 to Marksmanship)

*Provisions for three days – 10 lbs
The quality of food you get is determined during Episode 1.

> **Excellent:** Fresh beef, bacon, soft bread, potatoes, dried fruit, fresh vegetables, beans
>
> > (+1 to Health spins against Disease)
>
> **Good:** Salt beef, hard tack, dried fruit, fresh vegetables, beans, rice, cornmeal
>
> > (+0 to Health spins against Disease)
>
> **Poor:** Salt pork, hard tack, desiccated vegetables, dried fruit
>
> > (–1 to Health spins against Disease)

Other Equipment

*Ammunition – 10 shots per pound
Powder, lead balls, and paper cartridges

*Wool uniform – 7 lbs
Pants, cap, shirt, jacket, and coat

Bayonet – 2 lbs
Long knife that is attached to the end of a rifle or musket

Knapsack – 5 lbs
Leather backpack to carry supplies

Haversack – 2 lbs
Canvas bag to carry supplies

Woolen blanket – 3 lbs
Used for sleeping

Rubber blanket – 2 lbs
Waterproof blanket used to put on the ground or make a shelter

Shelter tent – 8 lbs
One-person tent for sleeping

Winter clothing – 7 lbs
Extra clothes for cold weather

Extra clothing – 3 lbs
Extra pants and shirt

Eating utensils – 2 lbs
Fork, spoon, knife, and tin cup

Sewing kit – 1 lb
Needle and thread to fix uniform

Grooming kit – 3 lbs
Brush, comb, hand mirror, shaving tools, toothbrush

Soap and towel – 2 lbs
Used for cleaning up before meals

Water purification kit – 5 lbs
Makes river and creek water clean to drink

Body armor – 10 lbs
Steel vest designed to protect the wearer

*Required items

Easy Simulations: Civil War © 2008 by Tim Bailey, Scholastic Teaching Resources

EQUIPMENT AND SUPPLIES FOR THE CONFEDERATE ARMY

***Weapons** – 10 lbs
The weapon you get is determined during Episode 1.

> **Good:** Enfield Rifle
> Well-made British rifle
>
> (+0 to Marksmanship)

> **Poor:** 1842 Smoothbore Musket
> 20-year-old musket
>
> (–1 to Marksmanship)

> **Terrible:** 1822 Smoothbore Musket
> This musket belongs in a museum
>
> (–2 to Marksmanship)

***Provisions** for three days – 10 lbs
The quality of food you get is determined during Episode 1.

> **Good:** Salt beef, hard tack, hominy, dried fruit, fresh vegetables, beans, cornmeal
>
> (+0 to Health spins against Disease)

> **Poor:** Salt pork, hard tack, dried fruit, desiccated vegetables, cornmeal
>
> (–1 to Health spins against Disease)

> **Terrible:** Rancid bacon, hard tack, cornmeal
>
> (–2 to Health spins against Disease)

Other Equipment

*Ammunition – 10 shots per pound
Powder, lead balls, and paper cartridges

*Cotton uniform – 4 lbs
Pants, cap, shirt, jacket, and coat

Bayonet – 2 lbs
Long knife that is attached to the end of a rifle or musket

Knapsack – 5 lbs
Leather backpack to carry supplies

Haversack – 2 lbs
Canvas bag to carry supplies

Cotton blanket – 2 lbs
Used for sleeping

Rubber blanket – 2 lbs
Waterproof blanket used to put on the ground or make a shelter

Shelter tent – 8 lbs
One-person tent for sleeping

Eating utensils – 2 lbs
Fork, spoon, knife, and tin cup

Sewing kit – 1 lb
Needle and thread to fix uniform

Grooming kit – 3 lbs
Brush, comb, hand mirror, shaving tools, toothbrush

Soap and towel – 2 lbs
Used for cleaning up before meals

Water purification kit – 5 lbs
Makes river and creek water clean to drink

Body armor – 10 lbs
Steel vests designed to protect the wearer

In addition, it was very common for Confederate soldiers to go without shoes, even in the winter, so each soldier must spin to see if he has shoes.

- If a soldier spins a number from 1 to 3, he has shoes.
- If a soldier spins a number from 4 to 6, he has no shoes.

*Required items

Easy Simulations: Civil War © 2008 by Tim Bailey, Scholastic Teaching Resources

MINOR INJURY TABLE

Spin once to determine the consequences of suffering a minor injury. After the effects of an injury have been determined, make another spin to see if there is a possible infection. You must spin a number equal to or lower than your Health number to avoid infection. If you spin a higher number, you must make a spin on the Infection Table.

If you spin . . .	You have . . .	Do this . . .
1	Bruised and cracked ribs – painful, but not serious, injury	Subtract 1 Health point, unless another soldier in the unit spins a number equal to or lower than his Medical Expertise number. Only one Medical Expertise spin can be attempted.
2	Small head laceration – a cut to the scalp that is not serious	Subtract 1 Health point, unless another soldier in the unit can stop the bleeding by spinning a number equal to or lower than her Medical Expertise number. Only one Medical Expertise spin can be attempted.
3	Flesh wound in the arm – metal passed through the muscle but not the bone or ligaments	Subtract 1 Health point, unless another soldier in the unit can bandage the injury by spinning a number equal to or lower than his Medical Expertise number. Only one Medical Expertise spin can be attempted.
4	Flesh wound in the leg – metal passed through the muscle but not the bone or ligaments	Subtract 1 Health point, unless another soldier in the unit can bandage the injury by spinning a number equal to or lower than her Medical Expertise number. Only one Medical Expertise spin can be attempted.
5	Dislocated shoulder – the soldier's arm has popped out of its socket	Subtract 1 Health point, unless another soldier in the unit can reduce the dislocation by spinning a number equal to or lower than his Medical Expertise number. Only one Medical Expertise spin can be attempted.
6	Broken foot – the soldier has broken a couple of bones in one foot	Subtract 1 Health point and 1 Agility point, unless another soldier can make a splint by spinning a number equal to or lower than her Medical Expertise number. If you are a Confederate soldier with no shoes, the soldier making the spin should subtract 1 from his Medical Expertise number before spinning.

MAJOR INJURY TABLE

Spin once to determine the consequences of suffering a major injury. After the effects of an injury have been determined, you must make a spin on the Infection Table.

If you spin . . .	You have . . .	Do this . . .
1 OR 2	Broken ribs and a punctured lung – a very serious wound that can result in serious infection and pneumonia	Subtract 2 Health points and 1 Stamina point due to bleeding and fluid filling up the punctured lung. To restore 1 Health point, another soldier in the unit must spin a number equal to or lower than her Medical Expertise number. Only one Medical Expertise spin can be attempted.
3 OR 4	Severe head wound – can be a tragic, often fatal injury	Subtract 3 Health points. If you survive this loss of Health points, spin again to determine the type of head wound: • If you spin 1 or 2, you lost one ear. • If you spin 3 or 4, you have a huge facial scar. • If you spin 5 or 6, you have been blinded. Soldiers who are blinded are sent home for the rest of the war. To restore 1 Health point, another soldier in the unit must spin a number equal to or lower than his Medical Expertise number. However, this cannot change the effects of being blinded. Only one Medical spin can be attempted.
5 OR 6	Traumatic limb injury – either an arm or leg has been severely injured, leaving the bone broken or even pulverized	Subtract 2 Health points. Spin again to determine which limb has been injured: • If you spin 1 or 2, you injured your left leg. • If you spin 3 or 4, you injured your right leg. • If you spin a 5, you injured your left arm. • If you spin a 6, you injured your right arm. To restore 1 Health point, another soldier in the unit must spin a number equal to or lower than her Medical Expertise number. If the Medical spin fails, the limb must be amputated and you lose 1 more Health point. If you survive this loss of Health points, you are sent home for the rest of the war.

Easy Simulations: Civil War © 2008 by Tim Bailey, Scholastic Teaching Resources

INFECTION TABLE

Spin once to see if an infection has developed from an injury. Infections and disease killed many more soldiers in the war than did bullets.

If you spin . . .	You have . . .	Do this . . .
1 OR 2	No infection – the soldier's own immune system has fought off the infection	
3 OR 4	Pneumonia – the injury has led to an infection in the lungs	Subtract 1 Health point. To keep you from losing additional Health points, another soldier in the unit must spin a number equal to or lower than his Medical Expertise number. If the spin fails, you lose 1 more Health point. A different soldier in the unit can attempt another Medical Expertise spin. This continues until either the Medical Expertise spin succeeds or you die of pneumonia.
5 OR 6	Streptococcus – the injury has turned septic. Often referred to as blood poisoning, sepsis killed many soldiers who appeared to be recovering from their wounds.	Subtract 2 Health points. To keep you from losing additional Health points, another soldier in the unit must spin a number equal to or lower than his Medical Expertise number. If the spin fails, you lose 1 more Health point. A different soldier in the unit can attempt another Medical Expertise spin. This continues until either the Medical Expertise spin succeeds or you die of infection.

DISEASE TABLE

Spin once to determine the consequences of contracting a disease. Many more soldiers died from disease and infection than from battlefield injuries.

If you spin . . .	You have . . .	Do this . . .
1 OR 2	Dysentery – a disease of the large intestine caused by an amoeba in unclean food or water. You begin to suffer from severe stomach cramps and diarrhea.	Subtract 1 Health point. To keep you from losing additional Health points, another soldier in the unit must spin a number equal to or lower than his Medical Expertise number. If the spin fails, you lose 1 more Health point and must subtract 1 point each from your Stamina and Strength numbers.
3 OR 4	Typhoid fever – contracted from body lice and other parasites. You get a high fever, spots on the skin, and intestinal bleeding.	Subtract 1 Health point. To keep you from losing additional Health points, another soldier in the unit must spin a number equal to or lower than his Medical Expertise number. If the spin fails, you become delirious and lose 1 more Health point. A different soldier in the unit can attempt another Medical Expertise spin. This continues until either the Medical Expertise spin succeeds or you die.
5 OR 6	Camp itch – a combination of heat rash and parasites. You are plagued by horrible itching.	No Health points are lost but you must make a Common Sense spin: • If you spin a number equal to or lower than your Common Sense number, you resist scratching and avoid infection. • If the spin fails, you lose 1 Health point due to the infections caused by scratching. To restore this lost Health point, another soldier in the unit must spin a number equal to or lower than her Medical Expertise number. Only one Medical Expertise spin can be attempted.

MORALE TABLE

The Morale number represents the emotional state of the soldier. A Morale of 5 shows a soldier who is in high spirits, eager to follow orders, and ready to attack the enemy. A Morale of 1 represents a soldier who is so emotionally fragile that he is ready to throw down his weapon and head for home. Morale can go up or down during the course of the simulation, but never above 5 or below 1. At certain times, specified during a scenario, you will be asked to make a Morale check. You will need to spin a number equal to or lower than your current Morale number in order to pass the check. If the spin fails, you must spin on the following Morale Table.

If you spin . . .	Then . . .
1	You find some source of inner strength that you didn't know you had. Raise your Morale by 1 point.
2	You are depressed and don't care about much. Lower your Morale by 1 point.
3	Things just seem to keep getting worse. Lower your Morale by 1 point.
4* *If this Morale Check is made during a battle, ignore this result and spin again.	You are irritable and argumentative. Randomly select someone else in your unit. Both of you must make a Common Sense spin: • If you both spin a number equal to or lower than your Common Sense number, you've succeeded in keeping your tempers. • If either of you spins a number higher than your Common Sense number, a fight has broken out, and the soldier with the lower Strength number loses 1 Health point. If your Strength numbers are equal, make a spin to see who got hurt during the fight. An even number means you were hurt, while an odd number indicates the other person got hurt. To restore the lost Health point, another soldier in the unit must spin a number equal to or lower than her Medical Expertise number.
5	You throw down your weapon and refuse to fight. If this occurs during a battle, you won't fight any more during that battle. If there is currently no battle, you refuse to follow the next order from a commander. Lower your Morale by 1 point.
6	You throw down your weapon and start running for home. After the battle, you can add 1 to your Morale and make another Morale Check. • If you spin a number equal to or lower than your Morale number, you return to your unit. • If you spin a number higher than your Morale number, you desert your unit and the army and head for home, hoping that you will not be caught and hanged for desertion.

Name: _____   Date: _____

RUBRIC #1
STUDENT'S JOURNAL

1 — Student did not record any events that occurred during the simulation.

2 — Student recorded very little about what occurred during the simulation.

3 — Student recorded information about what occurred during the simulation but in an incomplete fashion.

4 — Student recorded all of the important occurrences of the day's simulation, but not in a first-person narrative style.

5 — Student wrote detailed facts about the occurrences during the simulation and embellished these with personal thoughts in a believable first-person narrative style.

Score: _____

RUBRIC #2
TEACHER OBSERVATIONS

1 — Student was disruptive and prevented others from being able to participate in the simulation.

2 — Student did not participate in group discussions or simulation activities. Student might have been argumentative or disrespectful to other members of the group.

3 — Student either monopolized the group discussions or participated at a minimal level.

4 — Student participated well in the activity and allowed others to participate as well.

5 — Student was gracious in his or her participation and encouraged others to become engaged as well. Student role-played parts of the simulation to the best of his or her abilities.

Score: _____

RUBRIC #3
GROUP DYNAMICS

1 — Very poor. Members were fighting, sullen, ineffective.

2 — Poor. Members were arguing and generally ineffective, although they may have accomplished some of the simulation's tasks.

3 — Adequate. No real arguing or put downs of group members but not very supportive of one another. The simulation's tasks were completed by the group.

4 — Good. Effective use of group time and good support of group members.

5 — Great. Fantastic group participation as well as support from group members of one another. Group members all felt free to participate and contribute their ideas.

Score: _____

Total score: _____

Easy Simulations: Civil War © 2008 by Tim Bailey, Scholastic Teaching Resources

SIMULATION SPINNER

DIRECTIONS:

Use this spinner (or a number cube) at various points during the simulation to determine the outcome of a situation.

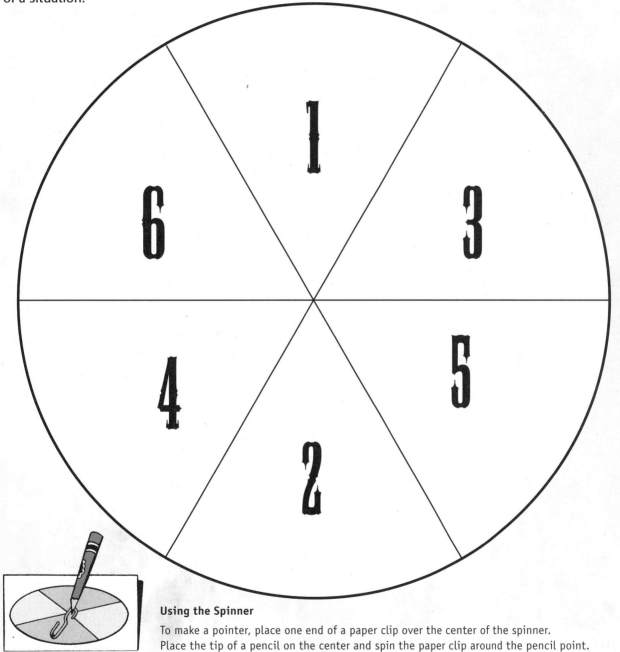

Using the Spinner

To make a pointer, place one end of a paper clip over the center of the spinner.

Place the tip of a pencil on the center and spin the paper clip around the pencil point.

Episode 1

WAR FEVER!

OVERVIEW

Students enlist in the army and are assigned to a regiment. They then spin the spinner to see what kind of weapons and provisions they get. Then they go through basic training and try to improve their skills to earn a promotion.

SCENARIO 1: JOINING UP!

If you haven't done so already, divide the class into two groups—Union soldiers and Confederate soldiers. Further divide each group into smaller units of four or five students. If you end up with an uneven number of units, give the Union the extra unit since the Union had more soldiers than the Confederacy.

Gather students together and read aloud the following passage:

April 17, 1862

It is an unusually hot day for April, but the sweat on your forehead has nothing to do with the sweltering heat. It doesn't help that the butterflies in your stomach feel as big as bats. You have decided to join the army and fight for your country! Rumors have been floating that soon the army will begin conscripting (drafting) men—and if you wait for that to happen, you may not have the choice of serving with your friends.

It has been a year since the battle at Fort Sumter triggered the war. You can still remember the headlines in the paper: "Bombing of Sumter!" "The War Commenced!" Now, you are standing in line at the county courthouse, waiting with your friends to get sworn into the army. In your mind, you can already envision how grand you will look in your new uniform . . . how proud your family will be . . . how exciting it will be to march into battle and defeat the enemy! Finally it is your turn to step forward and sign your name, or make your mark if you are illiterate, on your enlistment papers.

Invite each unit to come forward to find out which regiment they will be assigned to. Have each unit select a representative to spin the spinner. If a unit representative spins a number that has already been assigned, have that person spin again.

If you spin . . .	Union Regiments	Confederate Regiments
1	51st New York Infantry	53rd Alabama Infantry
2	10th Ohio Infantry	67th Georgia Infantry
3	33rd Pennsylvania Infantry	54th North Carolina Infantry
4	15th Maine Infantry	21st South Carolina Infantry
5	37th Massachusetts Infantry	35th Virginia Infantry
6	19th Connecticut Infantry	25th Mississippi Infantry

Have students write their new unit assignment in their journals. At this point, you might want to have each unit design a battle flag for their regiment (see References, page 64). Explain that during the war, each regiment designed its own battle flag and carried it into battle along with its national flag.

Tell students that they are now off to training camp where they will learn how to be soldiers!

SCENARIO 2: BASIC TRAINING—TURNING CIVILIANS INTO SOLDIERS

Read aloud the following passage:

April 23, 1862

You have arrived at the army camp where you will receive basic training. Your first introduction to military life is an inspection by the sergeant in charge of your training. He stands glaring at your group while chewing on his cigar for several minutes. Then he bellows, "How can they do this to me? Sent me a bunch of babies who will never be soldiers! I have never seen a more pathetic group of misfits in my life! Why, I'll bet you can't walk and chew at the same time, let alone learn to march and fight together! Oh well, I guess I'll just have to try and make soldiers out of you!" You are dismissed and assigned to your tent. You and the other soldiers in your unit will share a large tent in a muddy open field.

Next, it's time to get your uniform and find out what kind of weapons and provisions your unit will receive.

Invite each unit to send two representatives to make a spin—one for weapons and another for provisions. Before they make their spins, however, students can decide whether they want to try to talk the quartermaster (the officer in charge of supplies) into giving their unit the best available equipment. Each unit can try to improve either their weapons or their provisions, but not both. Give students a few minutes to decide with their units which one they would like to improve. After they have made their decision, have each unit pick a spokesperson to make a Common Sense spin to see if his unit succeeds in improving either their weapons or provisions.

- If the spokesperson spins a number equal to or lower than his Common Sense number, his unit can add 1 to the number that will be spun on either weapons or provisions, whichever his unit has decided upon. (For example, say a Union unit decided to improve their weapons, and the unit representative spins a 4. Adding 1 to that number makes it a 5, and the unit gets Springfield rifles instead of Enfield rifles. Of course, if the representative spins a 3, the added number will not make a difference.)

- If the spokesperson spins a number higher than his Common Sense number, his unit gets exactly the weapons and provisions that match the numbers their representatives will spin.

After all the units have made their Common Sense spin, have each unit's two representatives make a spin to see what kinds of weapons and provisions they get. Remember, if the unit's Common Sense spin was successful, add 1 to the number spun on either the weapons or provisions (depending on the unit's decision).

Choose Your Weapons		
If you spin . . .	**Union Weapons**	**Confederate Weapons**
1 or 2	1842 Smoothbore Musket (poor)	1822 Smoothbore Musket (terrible)
3 or 4	Enfield Rifle (good)	1842 Smoothbore Musket (poor)
5 or 6	Springfield Rifle (excellent)	Enfield Rifle (good)

Choose Your Provisions		
If you spin . . .	**Union**	**Confederate**
1 or 2	Poor Provisions	Terrible Provisions
3 or 4	Good Provisions	Poor Provisions
5 or 6	Excellent Provisions	Good Provisions

Read the following passage to students:

As new soldiers you soon discover that life in the military is an endless series of drills: marching, shooting, charging, and more marching.

Rules in the army are strict and discipline is rough. If a soldier breaks the rules, he is forced to march back and forth carrying a knapsack full of bricks or stand on top of a barrel for hours at a time. If anyone breaks one of the more serious rules, such as falling asleep while on sentry duty or committing desertion (running away from the army), he can be hanged!

Basic training has toughened both your mind and body and taught you the military skills that may save your life. During these six weeks of basic training, you may try and improve one of your skills (attributes).

(continued on next page)

(continued)

Choose the skill you would like to improve—Strength, Common Sense, Stamina, Marksmanship, Agility, or Medical Expertise. Keep in mind that the better you are now at a skill, the harder it will be to improve. In order to improve a skill you must spin a number higher than the one you already have. If you succeed, you can raise the skill number by one point. For example, Laura is a farmer who wants to improve her Agility. Her Agility number is 3, so she must spin a 4 or higher to raise the number by one point. Say, she spins a 5. Now she can raise her Agility number from 3 to 4. If she had spun 3 or lower, then her Agility would remain the same.

Invite soldiers to choose the skill that they wish to raise and then have them spin and adjust their numbers if they succeed. Continue reading to students:

One evening, after another exhausting day of drilling, the regimental commander comes to talk to the soldiers. Your drill sergeant yells, "Attention, snap to for the Colonel!" You and the rest of your unit jump up and stand stiff as boards with your eyes forward. The gray-bearded commander clears his throat and says, "When you arrived at this camp six weeks ago, I saw a bunch of farmers and tradesmen. Now as I look at you, I am proud to say that I see a regiment of soldiers. Tomorrow you will begin a journey that will take you to engage the enemy. Get a good night's rest and I will see you on the parade ground at reveille."

Inform students that at the end of boot camp, everyone receives his starting rank in the army. Anyone who showed exceptional ability during training may get promoted. Invite all of the soldiers who successfully raised one of their skill points to spin on the table at right to see what kind of promotion they received.

If you spin . . .	You are promoted to . . .
1 or 2	1st Private
3 or 4	Corporal
5 or 6	Sergeant

Students who did not raise any skill points during basic training start out as Privates. Have students record their rank in their journals.

JOURNAL PROMPT

Have students write about their experience as new recruits to the army. What was their training like? Is army life anything at all like what they expected it to be? How is it like or different from what they expected? How do they feel about their upcoming journey to meet the enemy?

Episode 2

"SHOUT THE BATTLE CRY OF FREEDOM!"

OVERVIEW

Students march toward the capital (Washington, D.C., for Union soldiers, or Richmond, Virginia, for Confederate soldiers) to hear their Commander-in-Chief give an inspiring speech, explaining the reasoning behind this War of the States. Afterward, they experience camp life as soldiers wait and get ready to march into battle.

SCENARIO 1: SPEECHES AND POLITICIANS

Have soldiers stand in formation with their units. Instruct the Union regiments to stand on one side of the room and the Confederate regiments to stand on the opposite side. Read aloud the following passage to the whole class:

May 30, 1862

The various regiments have embarked on a long march—toward the South for Union soldiers, and toward the North for Confederate soldiers. With your full kit strapped on and your weapon slung over your shoulder, you look like a soldier, even if you don't feel like one yet. You can't help but be excited that you are finally going to march into battle. After a 30-mile march in the scorching heat, however, you have lost much of your enthusiasm. Some of the soldiers are grumbling about the heat and want to stop and rest. But your orders specify that you must keep up this pace to meet the train that will be taking you to the capital (either to Washington, D.C., for Union soldiers or to Richmond, Virginia, for Confederate soldiers).

All soldiers in each unit must make a Stamina check to see how they are holding up during the march. (Remember, if a soldier is carrying more weight than his Strength limit [10 pounds for every Strength point], he must subtract 1 point from his Stamina number before making the following spin.)

- If a soldier spins a number equal to or lower than her Stamina number, she is doing fine.

- If a soldier spins a number higher than her Stamina number, she must lower her Morale by 1 point.

Have students adjust the numbers on their journal, if necessary.

Next, each unit must decide whether to stop and rest or march on. Allow students to discuss what their unit wants to do. Then invite a spokesperson from each unit to come up and tell you their decision. Make a note of it on a piece of paper. After you have every unit's decision, read them the following results:

1. If your unit decides to stop and rest, your spokesperson must make a spin to see if you were caught disobeying orders.

If you spin . . .	Then . . .
1 or 2	You enjoy a few peaceful moments of uninterrupted rest. Raise Morale for everyone in your unit by 1. (Remember: Morale cannot go above 5.)
3 or 4	You barely sit down before you see an officer coming. You jump up and resume marching. Your Morale stays the same.
5 or 6	Just as you close your eyes, you hear someone screaming at you for being a lazy, good-for-nothing soldier. You jump up as a captain bellows at you and threatens to put your unit on report! Subtract 1 Morale point from everyone in your unit.

2. If your unit decides to keep marching, you arrive at the train station on time only to find that the train is not there and will not arrive for another six hours! When the train finally arrives, you are loaded and packed into the boxcars. The boxcar doors are left wide open to allow for some air, and you begin the train ride to the capital city.

At this point, move toward the side of the room where the Union soldiers are standing and read them the following passage:

After spending two cramped days in a boxcar, the Northern soldiers arrive in Washington, D.C., to the cheers of a large crowd waiting at the train station. You are informed that you will be attending a speech given by President Abraham Lincoln at the White House that very afternoon. After washing up, you march down Pennsylvania Avenue to the White House where you are arranged, along with several other regiments, on the South Lawn of the White House. You see the newly erected

(continued on next page)

(continued)

platform from which the President will give his speech. An officer steps onto the platform and announces, "Ladies and gentlemen, the President of the United States of America." A tall, lanky man dressed in a black suit with a black bow tie steps across the lawn and onto the platform. He takes off the tall stovepipe hat that makes him look even taller than his 6-foot, 4-inch frame. His face is thin and gaunt, and his deep-set eyes look tired. He wears a beard without a mustache, reminding you that he is the first president ever to wear a beard in office. The crowd quiets down as the Commander-in-Chief begins to speak in a voice higher pitched than you had expected. He begins by welcoming the people of Washington and most especially you, the volunteer soldiers of the Union army. He then gets to the heart of his message, responding to recent criticism that he didn't really have a good reason for fighting the war and that he didn't know how to handle the issue of slavery:

"I would save the Union. I would save it the shortest way under the Constitution. The sooner the national authority can be restored; the nearer the Union will be 'the Union as it was.' If there be those who would not save the Union, unless they could at the same time save slavery, I do not agree with them. If there be those who would not save the Union unless they could at the same time destroy slavery,
I do not agree with them. My paramount object in this struggle is to save the Union, and is not either to save or destroy slavery. If I could save the Union without freeing any slave I would do it, and if I could save it by freeing all the slaves I would do it; and if I could save it by freeing some and leaving others alone I would also do that. What I do about slavery, and the colored race, I do because I believe it helps to save the Union; and what I forbear, I forbear because I do not believe it would help to save the Union. I shall do less whenever I shall believe what I am doing hurts the cause, and I shall do more whenever I shall believe doing more will help the cause. I shall try to correct errors when shown to be errors; and I shall adopt new views so fast as they shall appear to be true views. I have here stated my purpose according to my view of official duty; and I intend no modification of my oft-expressed personal wish that all men everywhere should be free."

The president's speech is greeted with cheering from the crowd. Looking around, however, you notice that there are those who did not seem to like President Lincoln's ideas about keeping or abolishing slavery.

> ### IT'S A FACT!
>
> This speech comes from a letter written by President Lincoln to the *New York Tribune* on August 22, 1862. It shows the president's view of his constitutional responsibilities and his personal feeling that slavery was wrong. At that time he was drafting the Emancipation Proclamation and would propose its adoption in the following months.

Next, move toward the Confederate soldiers on the opposite side of the room and read them the following passage:

The Southern soldiers find that their train ride north is short lived. After only one day of travel, the train was forced to stop because the tracks had been washed out by a flash flood.

From here you will have to walk to Richmond. The march is hot and dusty, but you finally reach the capital of the Confederacy. As you enter the town, young Southern belles in their huge hoop skirts greet you with cold drinks and praise for your bravery in going to fight those awful "Billy Yanks." While in town you hear that Jefferson Davis, President of the Confederacy, is giving a speech from the balcony of a hotel. You head in that direction to try to catch some of the speech.

As you squint up at the balcony, you see a man with wavy hair and a goatee standing at the railing. Despite the heat, he is wearing a vested suit with a full black bow tie. His face is thin and angular, and his hands grip the balcony railing as he speaks:

"Friends and Fellow Citizens, I thank you for the compliment that your presence conveys. It is an indication of regard, not for the person, but for the position which he holds. The cause in which we are engaged is the cause of the advocacy of rights to which we were born. Those for which our fathers of the Revolution bled: the richest inheritance that ever fell to man. And which is our sacred duty to transmit untarnished to our children. Upon us is devolved the high and holy responsibility of preserving the constitutional liberty of a free government. [The crowd around you breaks into applause.] Those with whom we have lately associated have shown themselves so incapable of appreciating the blessings of the glorious institutions they inherited that they are today stripped of the liberty to which they were born. They have allowed an ignorant usurper to trample upon all the prerogatives of citizenship, and to exercise power never delegated to him, and it has been reserved for your own state, so lately one of the original thirteen, but now, thank God, separated from them, to become the theatre of a great central camp, from which will pour thousands of brave hearts to roll back the tide of this despotism. [More wild cheering from the crowd] Upon every hill which now overlooks Richmond, you have had, and will continue to have, camps containing soldiers from every state in the Confederacy, and to its remotest limits every proud heart beats high with indignation at the thought that the foot of the invader has been set upon the soil of Old Virginia. [Great cheering all around you] There is not one true son of the South who is not ready to shoulder his musket to bleed, to die or to conquer in the cause of liberty here.

IT'S A FACT!

The South suffered from the very poor condition of its railroad system. The Union had a very extensive and reliable rail system. This was a major advantage for the North when it came to moving men and materiel.

IT'S A FACT!

This is an excerpt from a speech given June 1, 1861 at the Spotswood Hotel in Richmond by President Jefferson Davis.

The cheering is deafening all around you as you make your way out of the crowd and head to one of those army camps outside the city that President Davis has mentioned.

On your way back to camp you think about what Jefferson Davis has said. The Northerners are invaders trying to force the South to give up slavery and their precious way of life. The people of the North have been fooled by Abraham Lincoln, who wants to turn himself into some kind of king and force the people of America to do whatever he thinks is best, regardless of what the people really want. The gentle and fine way of life in the South is in danger of being destroyed by Lincoln and his Union invaders. You are going to make sure that does not happen.

Scenario 2: Camp Life

Read aloud the following passage to the whole class:

Your regimental commander privately informs you that you will begin the march toward enemy lines before dawn. This precautionary way of communicating ensures that the exact number of soldiers who will be heading out of camp is kept secret. After all, spies abound on both sides, making it difficult to keep troop movements a secret from the enemy.

The Colonel announces that he has asked the quartermaster to open his stores if you would like to exchange any of your equipment before the march begins early the next morning.

Allow students time to decide if they would like to get rid of or pick up different supplies based on their previous experience with marching. Have them let you know what they're keeping and what they're getting rid of, and instruct them to make the necessary changes in the supplies list in their journals.

Continue reading the following passage:

That night you sit around the campfire with the other soldiers in your unit. Many of the soldiers are either playing cards or writing letters home by firelight. Another soldier takes out a harmonica and begins to play a song. It's almost mealtime. To help prepare the meal, assign two soldiers from your unit to hike three miles to a stream to get water for washing up and making soup.

Have the two soldiers from each unit make a Strength spin to see if they can haul enough water back to camp.

- If both soldiers spin a number equal to or lower than their Strength number, they have successfully brought enough water for washing and preparing the meal.

- If either soldier spins a number higher than his Strength number, they fail to bring enough water. Every soldier in your unit must subtract 1 point from their Morale number because your unit has a very poor supper that evening.

For some time now, the regiments have been living on rations. Soldiers must make a Health spin to see if the rations are good enough to keep them healthy. If a soldier has soap or a grooming kit, however, he doesn't have to make a spin since these items will help keep him disease-free. Having a water purifier is just a waste because it doesn't work at all. (Remember, depending on the kind of provisions a soldier received in Episode 1 [i.e., excellent, good, poor, or terrible], she may have to adjust her Health number before making the following spin. See page 25 for Union soldiers and page 26 for Confederate soldiers.)

> ## In Their Own Words . . .
>
> You have no idea how dirty and irksome the camp life is . . . The weather is exceedingly hot and dusty. We send three miles for water. With most ablution [washing] is limited to face and hands, which rarely show the proper application of water. I write upon my knee, at present, as our table is otherwise employed.
>
> —James Chesnut, Jr. (written to his wife Mary, on June 22, 1861)

- If a soldier spins a number equal to or lower than her adjusted Health number, the rations keep her healthy and disease-free.

- If a soldier spins a number higher than her adjusted Health number, she must make another spin:

  → If she spins a number equal to or lower than her Health number on this second spin, she has caught a cold and loses 1 Health point. The good news is, she doesn't have to spin on the Disease Table.

  → If she spins a number higher than her Health number, she must make a spin on the Disease Table (page 30) and deal with the consequences.

Now, everyone needs to make a Morale spin due to the harsh conditions of camp life:

- If a soldier spins a number equal to or lower than his Morale number, he is doing fine.

- If a soldier spins a number higher than his current Morale number, he needs to spin on the Morale Table (page 31).

JOURNAL PROMPT

Have students write about their experiences from Episode 2. How did they feel after listening to their Commander-in-Chief's speech? Were they inspired or were they scared? How is camp life so far? Have them describe their day-to-day life in camp.

Episode 3

THE WINDS OF WAR

OVERVIEW

As students continue on their march toward the enemy, their nerves are tested by an unexpected encounter in the woods. How will they react? Later, they witness firsthand the after-effects of a battle and then weather a stormy night near the battlefield.

SCENARIO 1: A WALK IN THE WOODS

Inform students that they have been marching almost nonstop toward the enemy for the past three days. The marches have been long and hard, and they're beginning to take their toll on the soldiers. Everyone must make a Stamina spin to see how they are holding up.

- If a soldier spins a number equal to or lower than her Stamina number, she is doing just fine.

- If a soldier spins a number higher than her Stamina number, she must subtract 1 point from her Morale number.

After everyone has spun and those soldiers who need to have adjusted their Morale number, read aloud the following passage:

June 20, 1862

It is early afternoon as you march down a dirt road through a shadowy Virginia wood. Sunlight filtering through the leaves casts shadows across the road, and a slight breeze helps relieve the afternoon heat. Suddenly, you hear someone approaching. A curve in the road up ahead keeps you from seeing who or what is making the sound, but you know that the enemy lines are somewhere near. What will you do? Choose from the following options:

1. Load your weapons and fire at the approaching sound.

2. Hide off to the side of the road and wait to see who it is.

3. Send one of your soldiers up ahead to try to find out who is coming.

Allow soldiers to discuss their options within their units. Then invite a spokesperson from each unit to tell you the unit's decision, making sure to take note of it on a piece of paper. After all of the units have given you their decisions, read them the following results:

1. If your unit selected the first option and fired at the sound, subtract one round of ammunition from your supplies. The sound of your gunfire echoes through the woods, and the heavy smoke drifts into the trees. Up ahead you hear someone yell, "Stop shooting! I surrender!" You rush forward, expecting to take enemy prisoners. Instead, you find a cow riddled with bullet holes lying on the road and an old man crouching behind his dead cow! The old man jumps up when he sees you and starts yelling, "Are you all crazy? Why, you coulda killed me along with poor ol' Bess! Now what are you gonna do about my dead cow?" As you rack your brains trying to think what to say, your company commander rides up from behind you. He dismounts and looks at the dead cow. The captain glares at your unit with disgust and then steps forward to talk to the old man. After a short conversation, the old man seems to have calmed down. The captain informs you that you are to compensate him for the loss of his cow. Each soldier in your unit must give the old man an item from his or her supplies. In addition, everyone in the group must lower their Morale by 1 point. (Make sure students in the unit cross out something from their supplies list and tell you what it is. If you feel that they're not giving enough, you can make them give up more.)

2. If your unit chose to hide and wait to see what is coming down the road, everyone in your unit must make an Agility skill spin.

   - If a soldier spins a number equal to or lower than her Agility number, she was able to hide behind the trees before being spotted. The old man and his cow pass quietly by on the road, never knowing that the soldier was there.

   - If a soldier spins a number higher than her Agility number, the old man waves at her as he passes and says, "Afternoon. Nice day for a walk, eh?"

   If everyone in your unit makes the spin successfully, the company commander rides up and congratulates your unit on your quick thinking. Raise everyone's Morale by 1 point. If one or more soldiers miss the spin, everyone's Morale number stays the same.

3. If your unit decides to send a soldier to scout out who is coming down the road, that soldier must make an Agility skill spin.

   - If the soldier spins a number equal to or lower than his Agility number, he was able to move quietly through the woods without being spotted by the old man. The soldier returns to your unit and reports that the noise up ahead is just an old man and his cow. The company commander hears about your clever use of a scout and praises your unit. Raise everyone's Morale by 1 point.

- If the soldier spins a number higher than his Agility number, the old man hears the soldier in the woods. Pointing his walking stick at the soldier, the old man yells, "Hey, what do you think you're doing? Sneaking around in the woods and trying to scare a feller!"

SCENARIO 2: CROWS AND OTHER SCAVENGERS

Read aloud the following passage to the whole class:

June 21, 1862

As you emerge from the woods you see an open field ahead of you. You watch a flock of crows flap into the sky then settle again in the field. Next, you notice a group of men moving though the field, stooping and picking occasionally at something in the tall grass. As the wind shifts toward you, you detect the smell of death and decay. You suddenly realize that there was a battle fought here, probably in the last day or so. You can see that the men moving through the field are picking at the dead bodies, trying to find something they could use. You must decide what to do next:

1. March on and try to forget that soon you could be one of those dead bodies that the crows are picking at.

2. Stop and send two soldiers to go through the dead bodies and try to find better weapons than the ones you have now.

3. Stop and send two soldiers to go through the dead bodies and try to find better provisions than what you have now.

Allow soldiers to discuss their options within their units. Then invite a spokesperson from each unit to tell you the unit's decision, making sure to take note of it on a piece of paper. After all of the units have given you their decisions, read them the following results:

1. If you march on past the battlefield, you soon come to another field where you are ordered to set up camp for the night.

2. If you decide to stop and search for weapons, choose two soldiers to make a Common Sense spin:

- If either soldier spins a number equal to or lower than his Common Sense number, he has found weapons among the bodies. He should make another spin to see if the weapons are better than the ones your unit currently has.

➡ If he spins a number equal to or lower than his Common Sense number on this second spin, upgrade your unit's weapons by one grade. For example, if your unit had "poor" weapons, it now has "good" weapons. Only one upgrade is possible even if both soldiers are successful in their spins.

➡ If he spins a number higher than his Common Sense number on this second spin, he didn't find better weapons.

• If both soldiers spin a number higher than their Common Sense number on the first spin, neither one has found any weapons.

3. If you choose to stop and search for better provisions, choose two soldiers to make a Common Sense spin.

• If either soldier spins a number equal to or lower than her Common Sense number, she has found provisions among the bodies. She should make another spin to see if the provisions are better than the ones your unit currently has.

➡ If she spins a number equal to or lower than her Common Sense number on this second spin, upgrade your unit's provisions by one grade. For example, if your unit had "poor" provisions, it now has "good" provisions. Only one upgrade is possible even if both soldiers are successful in their spins.

➡ If she spins a number higher than her Common Sense number on this second spin, the provisions she has found are no better than the ones you already have.

• If both soldiers spin a number higher than their Common Sense number on the first spin, neither one has found any provisions.

After all the units have dealt with the consequences of their decisions, read the following passage:

The units that stopped to search through the dead bodies for weapons or provisions have to cope with seeing death up close for the first time. It is a grisly sight—one that you will never forget. It is already getting late as you head out of the battlefield and move toward the next field to camp out for the night. The other units that did not stop to scavenge have already set up their own camps.

For each unit that arrived earlier, choose up to three soldiers to make a Common Sense spin.

- If any of the soldiers spins a number equal to or lower than her Common Sense number, she notices storm clouds gathering in the distance and warns the unit.

- If all the soldiers spin a number higher than their Common Sense number, no one notices that a storm is coming.

For each unit that arrived late to camp, choose one soldier to make a Common Sense spin. For this spin, subtract 1 point from the soldier's Common Sense number as a penalty for arriving late.

- If a soldier spins a number equal to or lower than his Common Sense number (minus 1), he realizes that a big storm is coming and warns the rest of his unit.

- If a soldier spins a number higher than his Common Sense number (minus 1), he doesn't notice the ominous storm clouds.

IN THEIR OWN WORDS . . .

We had marched 10 miles when there came on the most severe electrical storm . . . It began with an awful display of lightening and thunder followed by intense darkness and a perfect deluge of rain . . . A real Hurrycane fell upon us . . . strewing trees and limbs on to our heads and filling the roads with debree . . . It was impossible for any one to see his hands before his eyes . . .

—W. H. H. Barker

Soon storm clouds gather, and lightning bolts blaze across the sky. Ear-splitting thunder shakes tree branches overhead, and sheets of rain mixed with hail pour from the sky. If a unit was successfully warned about the storm, they were able to make preparations and shelters. The unit can ride out the storm without much difficulty.

If a unit was caught in the storm without warning, the soldiers in that unit who do not have a tent must make a Health spin.

- If a soldier spins a number equal to or lower than her Health number, she avoids catching a chill from the wet weather.

- If a soldier spins a number higher than her Health number, she loses 1 Health point from getting soaked and catching a chill. However, if the soldier has an extra set of clothes, she does not lose the Health point.

A soldier who has a rubber blanket but no tent can make an extra Health spin if he missed the first one. If he succeeds in this second spin, he was able to use the rubber blanket for shelter and regain the lost Health point.

JOURNAL PROMPT

Have students write about what they experienced in Episode 3. What was it like to witness the after-effects of a battle? Have their feelings about the war changed? If so, how?

Episode 4

GOING TO SEE THE ELEPHANT

OVERVIEW

Students have their first encounter with the enemy. As they try to protect their own camp from enemy spies, they send out their own scout to spy on the other side. Then they have a skirmish with a cavalry unit from the enemy. Who will survive?

In this and the next episode, soldiers will see a great deal of combat. If a soldier is wounded, use the Minor or Major Injury Tables (pages 27–28) as indicated in the scenario and the Infection Table (page 29) when called for. (Make sure that anyone who receives a Major Injury also spins once on the Infection Table. Soldiers who incur a Minor Injury should make a Health spin to determine if they get infected or not.) If any soldier bought body armor and is still wearing it, he can ignore one injury during the simulation. After that, the body armor is useless. In addition, remind soldiers to subtract a round of ammunition every time they fire.

SCENARIO 1: PICKET DUTY AND GATHERING INTELLIGENCE

After grouping students by their units, read aloud the following passage to the class:

June 23, 1862

This afternoon your unit discovered that the enemy is camped in the woods ahead. You have occasionally heard the crack of gunfire in the distance and have even seen smoke—either from gunpowder or possibly campfires—drifting above the trees. Tonight the company commander has ordered that two soldiers from each unit be placed on picket duty. Picket duty means standing guard a few hundred yards from your army's camp and watching for a sneak attack by the enemy in the middle of the night. The soldiers on picket duty warn the rest of the army by firing on the enemy. Choose two soldiers from your unit to take picket duty for the night.

Allow students to discuss within their units who will be assigned to picket duty. Then invite a spokesperson from each unit to tell you who they chose and make a note of this.

Next, inform students that the commander has also asked that a soldier from each unit be chosen to sneak up on the enemy camp and spy on them. This soldier should gather as much information as possible and report back to the company commander. Allow the units to discuss and choose which soldier will spy on the enemy camp. Invite a spokesperson from each unit to tell you who they chose and make a note of this as well.

Ask the soldiers who have picket duty to come forward, and read them following passage:

As soldiers on picket duty, you are positioned in the woods near the edge of an open field. Across the field are the woods where the enemy is camped. Occasionally you get a glimpse of light that must be from the enemy's campfires. Moonlight helps you see out into the open field, but when clouds pass in front of the moon, the night turns pitch black. You cannot even see your hand held out in front of your face. You lean against a tree, trying desperately to stay awake when an owl overhead suddenly breaks the silence with a low hoot. You nearly jump out of your skin in fright. You hear a rustling in the trees off to your left. You freeze and squint to see what is moving. What will you do?

1. Don't take any chances. Fire your loaded gun at the sound to alert the army camp.

2. Wait and see if the sound gets closer so that you can get a better look.

3. Move toward the sound and try to get a better look.

Invite both soldiers on picket duty from each unit to tell you their combined decision and make a note of it. (If the soldiers can't agree, the higher-ranking soldier decides for both. If they are the same rank, have them make a spin, and the one with the higher number gets to decide.) After you have heard everyone's decision, read them the following results:

1. If you chose to fire, subtract a round of ammunition from your supplies and decide who will make a Marksmanship spin.

- If you spin a number equal to or lower than your Marksmanship number, you hear a muffled yell and the sound of someone falling into the bushes.

- If you spin a number higher than your Marksmanship number, you hear a voice yell, "Hey, I'm one of you! Just got lost on my way back to camp!" You can either shoot again or yell back to the person.

➡ If you shoot again, repeat the procedure above.

➡ If you decide to yell back, spin on your Common Sense:

♦ If you spin your Common Sense number or lower, you realize that the person is one of your own soldiers.

♦ If you spin a number higher than your Common Sense number, you fire at the person again because you believe that he is the enemy.

Repeat this series of events until either the other soldier has been shot or you realize that he is not the enemy.

When you investigate, you see that you have shot another soldier from your own army. Both soldiers on picket duty can attempt to save his life by spinning their Medical Expertise number or lower; if both spin a number higher than their Medical Expertise number, the soldier dies. If he lives, both soldiers lower their Morale by 1 point. If he dies, lower Morale by 2 points.

2. If you wait and see what is making the sound, decide who will make a Common Sense spin.

● If you spin a number equal to or lower than your Common Sense number, you realize that it is one of your own soldiers who had gotten lost in the woods.

● If you spin a number higher than your Common Sense number, you shoot at what you believe is an enemy soldier. Make a Marksmanship spin and follow the procedure detailed in the #1 result above.

3. If you move toward the sound, as you approach the sound stops. Then you hear the unmistakable sound of a musket being cocked and readied to fire. A flash of light in the dark nearly blinds you. Decide who will make an Agility spin.

● If you spin a number equal to or lower than your Agility number, the shot missed you. You can either return fire or duck under cover.

➡ If you decide to return fire, make a Marksmanship spin and proceed as in the #1 result explained above.

➡ If you stay under cover, the other soldier realizes that you are both in the same army and apologizes for nearly killing you.

● If you spin a number higher than your Agility number, spin again to see if your injury is major or minor.

➡ If you spin a number from 1 to 4, you suffer a minor wound. Make a spin on the Minor Injury Table to see what kind of wound you sustained and its consequences.

➡ If you spin a 5 or 6, you have a major wound. Make a spin on the Major Injury Table to see what kind of wound you sustained and its consequences.

Next, invite the soldiers who were chosen to spy to come forward, and read them the following passage:

You have been chosen to spy on the enemy camp. You set off in the direction of the campfires visible through the woods. First, try and sneak past the enemy's picket guards, who are stationed in the woods. Carefully pick your way through the underbrush and try not to make any noise that would give you away.

Make an Agility spin to see if you can move quietly through the woods.

- If you spin a number equal to or lower than your Agility number, you have successfully snuck past the picket and find yourself crouching behind a tree just outside the firelight of the enemy camp.

- If you spin a number higher than your Agility number, a guard on picket duty calls out, "Who goes there?" You hold your breath and wait to see if you are discovered. Make another Agility spin to see if you can hide from the soldier.

  → If you spin your Agility number or lower, the soldier passes by, thinking that you were just a porcupine or raccoon moving in the woods.

  → If you spin a number higher than your Agility number, the soldier shoots when he gets a good look at you in the moonlight. Make a spin to see what kind of wound you receive:

    ◆ If you spin a number from 1 to 4, you receive a minor wound. Make a spin on the Minor Injury Table to see what kind of wound you sustained and its consequences. If your injury is minor, you try to run away, but you must make a Stamina spin to see if you make it back to your own camp. If you spin your Stamina number or lower, you make it back safely. If you spin a number higher than your Stamina number, you have collapsed and have been captured. (For the purposes of this simulation, a soldier who has been captured is as good as dead. However, like a dead soldier, he must still participate as the "unseen conscious" of his unit.)

    ◆ If you spin a 5 or 6, you suffer a major wound. Make a spin on the Major Injury Table to see what kind of wound you sustained and its consequences. If your injury is major, you have been captured by the enemy and will be sent to a prisoner-of-war camp.

If you have successfully snuck into the enemy camp, begin counting the number of men, horses, and artillery pieces. After you have finished your count, you have to sneak back out of the camp and past the pickets. Repeat the process you used to sneak in, as described on the previous page. If you succeed in getting the information back to your own camp, raise your Morale by 2 points and everyone else's in your unit by 1 point.

SCENARIO 2: SKIRMISH

Read aloud the following passage to the whole class:

June 24, 1862

The morning dawns clear and bright. Your unit has been given orders to swing through the woods to the right and make sure that the enemy is not trying to flank your army. As you move through the woods, you hear the sound of horses and riders coming toward you at a walking pace. What do you do?

1. Load your weapons and fire at the approaching riders.

2. Hide among the trees and wait to see who is coming.

3. Send someone from your unit to see who is coming.

Allow soldiers to discuss their options within their units. Then invite a spokesperson from each unit to tell you the unit's decision, making sure to take note of it on a piece of paper. After all of the units have given you their decisions, read them the following results:

1. If you chose to fire at the approaching horses and riders, you discover that you have caught a detachment of the enemy's cavalry off guard. Everyone in your unit must make a Marksmanship spin. Remember to subtract a round of ammunition from your supplies.

- If a soldier spins her Marksmanship number or lower, she has hit one of the enemy cavalrymen.

- If a soldier spins a number higher than her Marksmanship number, she has missed.

If three or more soldiers from your unit hit their targets, the cavalry turns and gallops back the way they came. Raise the Morale of every soldier in your unit by 1 point. If fewer than three soldiers hit their targets, the cavalrymen return fire. Everyone in the unit must make an Agility spin.

- If a soldier spins his Agility number or lower, he takes cover and receives no injury.

- If a soldier spins a number higher than his Agility number, he has been injured. He must spin again to see if his wound is minor or major.

  → If a soldier spins a number from 1 to 4, he received a minor wound. He must spin on the Minor Injury Table to see what kind of wound he sustained and its consequences.

  → If a soldier spins a 5 or 6, he received a major wound. He must spin on the Major Injury Table to see what kind of wound he sustained and its consequences.

After returning fire, the cavalry gallops back to their own lines to report the encounter.

2. If you decided to hide in the woods and see who is coming, everyone in your unit must make an Agility spin. For this spin, however, each soldier must first subtract 1 point from her Agility number because a cavalryman on horseback can see farther than a man on foot.

- If every soldier in the unit spins their Agility number or lower, everyone has found a good hiding place. You soon find out that the approaching riders are a detachment of the enemy's cavalry. Proceed with the skirmish as described in the #1 result above, beginning with everyone in the unit making a Marksmanship spin. Remember to subtract a round of ammunition for each shot made.

- If any of the soldiers spins a number higher than her Agility number, the cavalrymen have spotted her and start firing at your unit. Everyone in the unit must make another Agility spin to take cover:

  → If a soldier spins his Agility number or lower, he successfully finds cover.

  → If a soldier spins a number higher than his Agility number, he has been injured. He must spin again to see what kind of wound he sustained.

    ◆ If a soldier spins a number from 1 to 4, he received a minor wound. He should spin on the Minor Injury Table to see what kind of wound he sustained and its consequences.

    ◆ If a soldier spins a 5 or 6, he received a major wound. He should spin on the Major Injury Table to see what kind of wound he sustained and its consequences.

3. If your unit decided to send a soldier to scout what is coming, choose who you will send. That soldier must then make an Agility spin. For this spin, however, the soldier must first subtract 1 point from his Agility number because a cavalryman on horseback can see farther than a man on foot.

- If the scout spins his Agility number or lower, he can report to the group that the enemy is coming and you can fire first as in the #1 result above. Repeat the same procedure as described.

- If the scout spins a number higher than his Agility number, the enemy has spotted him. He must now make a spin to see how many times he gets wounded by the enemy. (Obviously, a scout who is spotted by the cavalry is in deep trouble because he can be wounded up to six times!) After determining how many times he gets wounded, he must make a spin for each injury to see if it is minor or major.

  → If the scout spins a number from 1 to 4, he received a minor wound. He must spin on the Minor Injury Table to see what kind of wound he sustained and its consequences.

  → If the scout spins a 5 or 6, he received a major wound. He must spin on the Major Injury Table to see what kind of wound he sustained and its consequences.

After shooting the scout, the cavalry rides back to their camp to report that they encountered the enemy.

JOURNAL PROMPT

Have students write in their journals about the events in this episode. Remind them to write in character, even if their character has died or been captured.

Episode 5

"HE HATH LOOSED THE FATEFUL LIGHTNINGS OF HIS TERRIBLE SWIFT SWORD"

OVERVIEW

Students finally get to experience an actual battle. This episode is based on a battle that took place during Union General George McClellan's campaign to defeat Confederate General Robert E. Lee and to capture the Confederate capital of Richmond, Virginia, in 1862.

As in the previous episode, make sure students have the Minor and Major Injury Tables and the Infection Table at hand.

SCENARIO 1: PREPARING TO LIVE AND DIE

After grouping students by their units, read aloud the following passage to the class:

June 25, 1862

Another beautiful dawn breaks, and birds are singing in the swampy meadow that lies between the groves of trees where the opposing armies are camped. In his tent, General Robert E. Lee, commander of the Confederate army, is planning a defense against an attack he expects to happen before the end of the day. He is convinced that the Union army is trying to move its siege artillery within range of the Confederate capital city of Richmond. Both armies are already so close to Richmond that Lee can hear the city's church bells ringing in the clear morning air. He orders defenses to be built to repel an attack by the numerically superior Union army. Lee is surprised that the Union army has not yet struck, but the commander of the Union army, General George McClellan, is waiting for his own reinforcements to arrive, even though he already has a sizable advantage in men and weaponry.

The Confederate units need to build several kinds of defenses quickly. They need to dig trenches and use the dirt to construct *embankments* (dirt piled up to hide from behind). They need to chop down trees to build an *abatis* (a network of cut trees to slow down the enemy) and to make *palisades* (sharpened sticks with points sticking up from the ground).

To see if the Confederate army has successfully built their defenses, have every Confederate soldier come forward to make both a Strength and a Stamina spin.

- If a soldier spins a number equal to or lower than her Strength number or her Stamina number, the spin is successful. For every successful spin, a soldier can ignore one injury in the upcoming battle (up to two injuries, if both spins are successful).

- If on both attempts a soldier spins a number higher than her Strength or Stamina number, the defense she's hiding behind is not strong enough to protect her. The soldier is just as vulnerable as if she were standing out in the open.

SCENARIO 2: THE BATTLE OF OAK GROVE

Have the Union regiments and Confederate regiments stand in formation on opposite sides of the room. In this scenario, the narrative goes back and forth between the North and South. Each section of the narrative will be labeled "Union Army" or "Confederate Army," depending on which side is supposed to take action during that particular section. In other words, if a spin is required in a section labeled "Union Army," only Union soldiers are supposed to make the spin.

Read aloud the following passages:

Union Army

June 25, 1862

The Battle of Oak Grove begins with a massive artillery barrage by the Union army. General George McClellan, commander of the Union army, has ordered his cannons to blast the newly built Southern defenses. With their greater range, the Union cannons start blasting away from their side of the woods in the early afternoon. In the meantime, the Union soldiers  are massed in the woods at the edge of the woods, waiting for the signal to advance across the open meadow.

You look around at the nervous, sweaty faces of the other soldiers and check your weapon and ammunition for the hundredth time. The booming of the cannons behind you startles you. You see huge spouts of dirt shoot into the air where the Confederates have built their defenses. The order to advance should be coming soon.

Confederate Army

The Battle of Oak Grove begins with the sight of cannon smoke puffing from the woods across the meadow. A few seconds later the shrill scream of an incoming cannonball has everyone diving into the trenches for cover. The earth shakes as the cannonballs crash and explode. The barrage of cannon fire increases in intensity as the Union artillery finds the exact range to the Confederate defense. Dirt flies into the air and shattered palisades spin in every direction. Splintered logs turn into deadly shrapnel, shredding everything around them.

All Confederate soldiers must make a Common Sense spin as they try to take cover from flying shrapnel.

- If a soldier spins his Common Sense number or lower, he has avoided injury.

- If a soldier spins a number higher than his Common Sense number, he has been hit by flying shrapnel. (Remember, a soldier who has made a successful Strength and/or Stamina spin in the first scenario can ignore up to two injuries.) The wounded soldier must make another spin to see how severe the injury is.

  ➡ If a soldier spins a number from 1 to 4, the injury is minor. He makes a spin on the Minor Injury Table to see what kind of wound he sustained and its consequences.

  ➡ If a soldier spins a 5 or 6, the injury is major. He makes a spin on the Major Injury Table to see what kind of wound he sustained and its consequences.

All Confederate soldiers now need to make a Morale spin.

- If a soldier spins her Morale number or lower, her Morale stays the same.

- If a soldier spins a number higher than her Morale number, she must make a spin on the Morale Table.

After what seems like an eternity, the cannon fire slows. You peak over the embankment and see the Union army's blue-uniformed infantry beginning to march out of the woods and cross the grassy meadow.

Union Army

"Advance!" the Union major yells, pointing his sword toward the Confederate embankments. The long rows of soldiers begin to march across the meadow. A couple of overanxious rebels fire at your lines, but you are still out of range. Advancing in neat rows, your regiment approaches the swift running creek that cuts across the meadow. The major orders, "Double time!" and your regiment breaks into a trot. Suddenly you see big, bright flashes and clouds of smoke as the

Confederate artillery opens fire on the rows of blue-jacketed Union soldiers. Cannonballs thunder into the earth around you, and deadly pieces of hot metal explode into the air along with dirt and bodies of blasted soldiers.

All Union soldiers must make an Agility spin to try to avoid getting wounded by the cannon fire.

- If a soldier spins her Agility number or lower, she has avoided injury.

- If a soldier spins a number higher than her Agility number, she has been wounded by cannon fire. The wounded soldier must make another spin to see how severe the injury is.

  ➡ If a soldier spins a number from 1 to 4, the injury is minor. She makes a spin on the Minor Injury Table to see what kind of wound she sustained and its consequences.

  ➡ If a soldier spins a 5 or 6, the injury is major. She makes a spin on the Major Injury Table to see what kind of wound she sustained and its consequences.

As you look around for the major, all you find is what's left of the feathered hat he was wearing. A captain is now waving his sword and screaming, "Charge!" even though your regiment is still several hundred yards from the enemy's embankments. You leap over the creek and scramble up the other side. You stop, drop to your knee, and fire.

All Union soldiers must make a Marksmanship spin to see if they hit their target.

- If a soldier spins his Marksmanship number or less, he has shot down his target. He can disregard the next wound he receives because he has hit the soldier who would have shot him.

- If a soldier spins a number higher than his Marksmanship number, he has missed his target.

Confederate Army

You watch as the straight lines of Union soldiers advance in perfect formation across the field, the brass buttons on their handsome blue uniforms glinting in the afternoon sun. These perfect lines soon falter as your regiment's cannons blast the Northerners with cannonballs and canister rounds. The canister rounds are like giant shotgun shells that spray hundreds of metal pieces or even bits of chain and glass. Even as holes form in the Union lines, more soldiers come up to fill in the gaps. Soon the Billy Yanks are trotting toward you and beginning to fire randomly at your defenses. You hear your regiment's colonel yell, "Steady men, let them come on. Steady. Steady. All right, let 'em have it! Fire!"

All Confederate soldiers must make a Marksmanship spin to see if they hit their target.

- If a soldier spins her Marksmanship number or less, she has shot down her target. She can disregard the next wound she receives because she has hit the soldier who would have shot her.

- If a soldier spins a number higher than her Marksmanship number, she has missed her target.

Union Army

As Union soldiers run toward the enemy, the entire front of the Confederate embankments is suddenly shrouded in smoke. The gunfire from the Confederate troops is deadly, and Union soldiers are mowed down like wheat.

All Union soldiers must make an Agility spin to try to avoid getting wounded.

- If a soldier spins his Agility number or lower, he has avoided injury.

- If a soldier spins a number higher than his Agility number, he has been wounded. The wounded soldier must make another spin to determine the extent of his injury.

  ⇒ If a soldier spins a number from 1 to 4, the injury is minor. He makes a spin on the Minor Injury Table to see what kind of wound he sustained and its consequences.

  ⇒ If a soldier spins a 5 or 6, the injury is major. He makes a spin on the Major Injury Table to see what kind of wound he sustained and its consequences.

All Union soldiers now need to make a Morale spin.

- If a soldier spins her Morale number or lower, her Morale stays the same.

- If a soldier spins a number higher than her Morale number, she must make a spin on the Morale Table.

Confederate Army

The Confederate commanders want to try to break the back of the Union charge with a charge of their own. You hear the order being repeated up and down the line: "Fix bayonets!" You quickly attach a long blade to the end of your musket and prepare to leap over the embankment and meet the enemy hand-to-hand. The colonel stands above the embankment, ignoring the bullets that whiz past him, and gives the order, "Charge!" You come charging over the embankment and run toward the enemy, holding your musket low at your hip and ready to thrust with the bayonet. As you approach the enemy, you and your fellow soldiers let out the famous "rebel yell."

Union Army

You see the gray-uniformed Southerners burst out of the embankments with their bayoneted muskets held in front of them. As they charge toward you, they begin screaming and hollering like demons!

All Union soldiers must make a Morale spin.

- If a soldier spins his Morale number or lower, his Morale stays the same.

- If a soldier spins a number higher than his Morale number, he must make a spin on the Morale Table.

The captain yells "Retreat!" and you begin backing away from the charging enemy and seek the cover of the creek embankment behind you.

Confederate Army

The Union army is in full retreat as you charge toward them, but they quit running when they reach the cover offered by the creek embankment. The bugle sounds the retreat for your own troops and you scramble back to the safety of your defenses.

As the afternoon wears on, the battle winds down until both sides find themselves pretty much where they started the day. The sight of dead bodies, the moans of the wounded, and the smell of gunpowder fill your senses. As the sun begins to set, the wounded are carried back to the two camps. The business of war has ended for the day.

JOURNAL PROMPT

Have students write in their journals about the events in this episode. What did it feel like to be in an actual battle? How does it compare to how they felt when they first signed up for the army? Remind students to write in character, even if their character has died.